TIME TO COMPARE!

Which HAS MORE?

T0009815

BY JAGGER YOUSSEF

Gareth Stevens
PUBLISHING

first concepts

We can compare!
The girl has
more books.

3

The boy has
more flowers.

The bowl has
more pasta.

The basket has more grapes.

9

The box has
more sand.

11

The bucket has
more popcorn.

13

The bag has
more food.

15

The red plate has
more cookies.

The left tree has more apples.

19

The right tree has more oranges.

Point to the box
that has more toys.